EMMANUEL JOSEPH

Hamas and International Relations: Allies and Alliances

First edition

This book was professionally typeset on Reedsy.
Find out more at reedsy.com

Contents

1

Chapter 1: Introduction: Understanding Hamas and Its Global Significance

C hapter Overview:

This introductory chapter sets the stage for the book, "Hamas and International Relations: Allies and Alliances," by providing readers with a fundamental understanding of Hamas and its significance in the global political landscape. It outlines the key objectives and scope of the book, explains the relevance of studying Hamas in the context of international relations, and offers a glimpse of the major themes that will be explored in the subsequent chapters.

Introduction:

Hamas, or the Islamic Resistance Movement, is an organization that has consistently captured the attention of the international community. It emerged in the late 1980s, primarily as a response to the Israeli occupation of Palestinian territories, and has since evolved into a multifaceted entity with global implications. Understanding Hamas is not merely an exercise in comprehending Palestinian politics; it is an exploration of the complex interplay between regional, international, and transnational actors in a conflict-ridden world.

This introductory chapter aims to provide a roadmap for our journey through the intricate world of Hamas and its international relations. The following sections will outline the primary objectives, the scope of the book, and the rationale behind delving into the subject matter.

Objectives:

1. To Analyze Hamas's Historical Evolution: We will delve into the historical roots of Hamas, exploring its founding, early motivations, and how it transformed into a prominent player in regional politics. This analysis is crucial for understanding its current global significance.

2. To Examine Hamas's Regional and International Alliances: Hamas's ties with regional actors like Iran, Turkey, and Qatar have reshaped the geopolitical landscape. This chapter introduces the key alliances we'll explore throughout the book and their impact on international relations.

3. To Assess the Role of Hamas in Broader Conflict Dynamics: Understanding Hamas is central to comprehending the Israeli-Palestinian conflict, Middle Eastern geopolitics, and global terrorism. We'll establish the importance of Hamas in these contexts.

Scope of the Book:

"Hamas and International Relations: Allies and Alliances" takes a multidisciplinary approach, drawing on political science, international relations, history, and sociology to analyze the multifaceted nature of Hamas. It explores the following areas:

- The origins and evolution of Hamas as a Palestinian resistance movement.
  - Hamas's relationship with regional powers, such as Iran, Turkey, and

Qatar, and the implications for regional dynamics.

- Western countries' policies towards Hamas, including their efforts to engage or isolate the organization.

- Hamas's interactions with non-state actors, such as Hezbollah, and how these connections influence international relations.

- The potential future scenarios for Hamas and its role in the ever-changing landscape of international politics.

Rationale:

Studying Hamas in the realm of international relations is imperative due to its far-reaching implications. The organization's actions and alliances influence not only the Israel-Palestine conflict but also the broader Middle East and even global politics. Understanding Hamas's motivations, strategies, and relationships with other international actors is a prerequisite for comprehending contemporary geopolitics and the interconnectedness of conflicts worldwide.

As we embark on this exploration of Hamas and its international relations, this chapter serves as a foundation, setting the context and expectations for the chapters to come. With a focus on historical evolution, regional alliances, and broader conflict dynamics, this book aims to provide a comprehensive understanding of the global significance of Hamas in the 21st century.

2

Chapter 2: Historical Roots of Hamas: From Founding to Transformation

Chapter Overview:
In this chapter, we delve into the historical evolution of Hamas, tracing its origins as a Palestinian resistance movement and its transformation into a multifaceted organization. Understanding Hamas's roots is essential for comprehending its current role in international relations and the broader geopolitical landscape.

Introduction:

Hamas's history is deeply entwined with the Palestinian struggle for statehood and self-determination. Founded in the late 1980s, it emerged as a response to the Israeli occupation of Palestinian territories. To understand the contemporary significance of Hamas in international relations, we must explore the organization's journey from its inception to its current status as a prominent player on the global stage.

Founding of Hamas:

Hamas was established in the late 1980s during the First Intifada, a Palestinian uprising against Israeli rule. Its founders, including Sheikh Ahmed Yassin and Mahmoud Al-Mabhouh, were influenced by various factors, including religious ideologies and a desire to resist the Israeli occupation. The organization's early days were marked by grassroots activism, providing social services, and challenging Israeli authority through both non-violent and violent means.

Evolution of Hamas:

Hamas underwent a significant transformation in the 1990s, following the Oslo Accords and the establishment of the Palestinian Authority. The organization began to consolidate its power in the Gaza Strip and West Bank. This evolution included participating in Palestinian elections and winning seats in the Palestinian Legislative Council.

Violence and Resistance:

Hamas's use of violence, including suicide bombings and rocket attacks, garnered international attention and condemnation. Its tactics were driven by its opposition to the Oslo Accords and a belief in armed resistance as a means to achieve Palestinian self-determination.

Hamas and the Israeli-Palestinian Conflict:

Hamas's role in the conflict with Israel has been central to its historical trajectory. The organization's stance on issues like the right of return for Palestinian refugees, the status of Jerusalem, and the boundaries of a future Palestinian state have shaped the dynamics of the Israeli-Palestinian conflict.

Global Impact:

As Hamas continued to evolve, its actions and ideology attracted attention and support from regional and international actors. Its role in the wider Middle East and its alliances with countries like Iran have had profound implications for global geopolitics.

This chapter lays the foundation for the subsequent exploration of Hamas's international relations. It is essential to understand the historical roots of Hamas to make sense of its alliances, actions, and its enduring significance on the international stage. As we move forward in the book, we will examine how these historical developments have shaped Hamas's relationships with regional and international actors.

3

Chapter 3: Hamas and Regional Dynamics: A Changing Landscape

C hapter Overview:

This chapter delves into the complex regional dynamics that have shaped Hamas's role and alliances. It explores how Hamas has adapted to a shifting geopolitical landscape and examines the organization's interactions with various regional actors.

Introduction:

The Middle East is a region characterized by its intricate web of alliances, conflicts, and shifting political landscapes. Hamas, as a Palestinian resistance movement and political entity, has been deeply influenced by these dynamics. In this chapter, we will examine how regional factors, including changes in leadership, conflicts, and strategic shifts, have shaped Hamas's role and its alliances.

The Regional Context:

To understand Hamas's position in the Middle East, it's essential to grasp the broader regional context. This includes the Arab-Israeli conflict, the Arab Spring, the rise of Islamist movements, and the enduring tensions between Sunni and Shia powers.

Hamas and the Palestinian Territories:

Hamas's influence in the Palestinian territories, particularly in the Gaza Strip, has created a dynamic interplay with the Palestinian Authority, Fatah, and the broader Palestinian political landscape. We'll explore the rivalry, cooperation, and power struggles that have defined these relationships.

Hamas and Israel:

The ongoing Israeli-Palestinian conflict remains a central aspect of regional dynamics. We'll discuss how Hamas's tactics and strategies have affected this conflict, including its role in ceasefire negotiations and its influence on the peace process.

Hamas and Egypt:

Egypt's role in mediating between Hamas and Israel and its control of the Rafah border crossing have been instrumental in the dynamics of the Gaza Strip. We'll examine how Egypt's policies have influenced Hamas's alliances and actions.

Hamas and the Gulf States:

The Gulf states, including Qatar and the United Arab Emirates, have played a significant role in supporting Hamas financially and politically. We'll explore the motivations and implications of these alliances.

The Impact of the Syrian Civil War:

The Syrian conflict posed a significant challenge to Hamas, leading to a reevaluation of its regional alliances. We'll analyze how the organization navigated the complexities of the Syrian civil war.

Hamas's Adaptation to Regional Changes:

Hamas has demonstrated an ability to adapt to changing regional dynamics. We'll examine its strategies for survival and growth, including its forays into international diplomacy and participation in Palestinian elections.

The Ongoing Yemen Conflict:

The Yemeni conflict has further complicated regional dynamics, impacting Hamas's relationships with regional actors, including Iran and Saudi Arabia.

Conclusion:

This chapter sheds light on the evolving regional landscape in which Hamas operates. It illustrates how the organization's alliances and actions have been shaped by regional factors, and it serves as a foundation for understanding the complex interplay between Hamas and various regional actors. In the following chapters, we will delve deeper into Hamas's specific alliances with countries such as Iran, Turkey, and Qatar, and their impact on international relations.

4

Chapter 4: Hamas and Iran: An Enduring Partnership

Chapter Overview:

In this chapter, we explore the deep-rooted and enduring partnership between Hamas and Iran. We examine the ideological and strategic dimensions of this relationship and its implications for both Hamas and international relations.

Introduction:

The relationship between Hamas, a Sunni Palestinian organization, and Iran, a predominantly Shia nation, might seem paradoxical on the surface. However, this chapter delves into the complexities of their alliance, highlighting the shared interests and ideological motivations that have sustained this partnership.

Historical Context:

The alliance between Hamas and Iran dates back to the early 1990s, a time when both entities were in need of regional allies. Iran, looking to expand its influence in the Middle East, saw Hamas as a valuable asset in its conflict with Israel and a means of promoting its own regional agenda.

Shared Ideological Grounds:

While Hamas is a Sunni organization and Iran is predominantly Shia, they have found common ground in their opposition to Israel and the Western powers. This chapter examines how their shared anti-Israel stance has been a unifying factor in their alliance.

Financial and Military Support:

Iran has provided substantial financial and military support to Hamas over the years. We'll explore how this support has influenced Hamas's military capabilities and its ability to resist Israeli forces.

Diplomatic and Political Cooperation:

Beyond financial and military assistance, the Hamas-Iran relationship includes diplomatic and political cooperation. Iran has advocated for Hamas on the international stage, further legitimizing the organization's role in Palestinian politics.

Regional Implications:

The Hamas-Iran alliance has significant regional implications, impacting not only the Israeli-Palestinian conflict but also the broader balance of power in the Middle East. We'll analyze how this alliance has shaped regional dynamics and conflicts.

Challenges and Tensions:

While the partnership has endured, it has not been without challenges and tensions. We'll discuss how regional developments, such as the Syrian civil war, affected the Hamas-Iran relationship and how both parties have navigated these complexities.

The Broader Geopolitical Landscape:

The Hamas-Iran alliance is a key element in the broader regional power struggles between Iran and its rivals, including Saudi Arabia and Israel. We'll examine how this alliance fits into the geopolitical puzzle of the Middle East.

Future Prospects:

As the geopolitical landscape in the Middle East continues to evolve, we'll consider the potential future scenarios for the Hamas-Iran alliance and its implications for international relations.

This chapter provides an in-depth analysis of the Hamas-Iran partnership, shedding light on the ideological, strategic, and regional dimensions of this relationship. It serves as a critical case study of how non-state actors form alliances with powerful states and their influence on international relations.

5

Chapter 5: The Qatar Connection: Financial and Political Support

C hapter Overview:
This chapter delves into the relationship between Hamas and the State of Qatar. It focuses on the significant financial and political support provided by Qatar to Hamas, and how this support has influenced the organization's policies and international relations.

Introduction:

Qatar's role in the Middle East has been marked by a willingness to support various Islamist movements, including Hamas. This chapter explores how Qatar's support for Hamas, both financially and politically, has played a pivotal role in the organization's evolution and international relations.

Qatar's Motivations:

To understand the Qatar-Hamas connection, we first examine Qatar's motivations for supporting Hamas. This includes a desire to bolster its position in regional politics, challenge regional rivals, and promote its own ideological agenda.

Financial Aid:

Qatar has provided substantial financial support to Hamas, particularly in the form of humanitarian assistance and infrastructure development in the Gaza Strip. We analyze the impact of this aid on the economic and social landscape of the Palestinian territories.

Political Backing:

Qatar has not only provided financial support but also offered political backing to Hamas. This includes hosting Hamas leaders and participating in diplomatic efforts aimed at resolving the Israeli-Palestinian conflict.

Implications for the Middle East:

Qatar's support for Hamas has had wider implications for the Middle East, including regional power struggles, rivalries with Saudi Arabia, and Qatar's role in the Gulf Cooperation Council (GCC). We explore how this support has shaped regional dynamics.

Hamas's Policies:

Qatar's support has influenced Hamas's policies, both in terms of its stance on regional issues and its approach to international relations. We'll discuss how this support has allowed Hamas to maintain its resilience and pursue its strategic objectives.

Challenges and Controversies:

The Qatar-Hamas connection has not been without challenges, including criticism from other Gulf states and the broader international community.

We examine how these controversies have affected Qatar's support for Hamas and Hamas's international image.

Diplomatic Initiatives:

Qatar has been involved in various diplomatic initiatives related to the Israeli-Palestinian conflict. We analyze how Qatar's role in these efforts has influenced the prospects for peace in the region and the status of Hamas in international relations.

Future Scenarios:

As the Middle East continues to evolve, we consider the potential future scenarios for the Qatar-Hamas relationship and its implications for the broader international landscape.

This chapter provides a comprehensive examination of the Qatar-Hamas connection, shedding light on the financial and political support provided by Qatar to Hamas and its far-reaching consequences for both the organization and international relations in the Middle East.

6

Chapter 6: Hamas and the Arab Spring: Impacts and Adaptations

Chapter Overview:
This chapter delves into the effects of the Arab Spring on Hamas and how the organization adapted to the changing regional landscape. It examines the challenges and opportunities presented by the uprisings in the Middle East and North Africa.

Introduction:

The Arab Spring, a series of uprisings that swept across the Middle East and North Africa, had a profound impact on the region's political dynamics. This chapter explores how Hamas navigated the challenges and opportunities that arose during this transformative period.

The Arab Spring: A Regional Transformation:

We begin by setting the stage with an overview of the Arab Spring and the political changes it brought to various countries, including Egypt, Tunisia, and Syria.

Hamas's Initial Response:

Hamas initially welcomed the Arab Spring and the rise of Islamist movements in the region. We'll discuss how these developments were seen as an opportunity for the organization to strengthen its regional position.

Challenges and Shifting Alliances:

As the Arab Spring evolved, so did the challenges for Hamas. We explore the complexities of managing alliances with regional actors such as the Muslim Brotherhood in Egypt, whose fortunes fluctuated during this period.

The Fall of the Muslim Brotherhood in Egypt:

The ousting of President Mohamed Morsi and the Muslim Brotherhood in Egypt presented a significant setback for Hamas. We analyze how this event influenced Hamas's regional relations and led to isolation in the Gaza Strip.

The Syrian Civil War: A Thorny Dilemma:

The Syrian conflict posed a particular dilemma for Hamas, given its long-standing relationship with the Syrian regime and its support for the opposition. We'll discuss how Hamas navigated this challenging situation.

Diversifying International Relations:

In response to the regional turbulence, Hamas sought to diversify its international relations. We examine how this led to engagement with various actors, including Iran, Qatar, and Turkey.

Impact on the Israeli-Palestinian Conflict:

The changing dynamics in the region had repercussions for the Israeli-

Palestinian conflict. We'll explore how shifts in Hamas's alliances and policies influenced its role in this long-standing conflict.

Adaptations and Survival Strategies:

Hamas's ability to adapt to the changing regional landscape and the challenges it faced is a central theme in this chapter. We analyze the strategies the organization employed to maintain its relevance and influence.

Conclusion:

The Arab Spring presented both opportunities and challenges for Hamas. This chapter provides insights into how the organization adapted to the shifting regional dynamics and navigated the complexities of the post-Arab Spring Middle East. It also serves as a bridge to understanding how these adaptations influenced its international alliances and the broader geopolitical context.

7

Chapter 7: Balancing Act: Hamas and Turkey's Involvement

Chapter Overview:

This chapter delves into the relationship between Hamas and Turkey, exploring the multifaceted nature of their interaction. It discusses the historical context, the various dimensions of their partnership, and the implications for international relations in the Middle East.

Introduction:

Turkey's involvement with Hamas is a complex and evolving relationship. This chapter aims to unravel the intricacies of this partnership, highlighting Turkey's motivations and the impact of its support on Hamas and international relations.

Historical Context:

The chapter begins by providing historical context, outlining the evolution of Turkey's approach to the Palestinian-Israeli conflict and its stance toward Hamas over the years.

Motivations for Turkish Involvement:

We examine Turkey's motivations for supporting Hamas, considering factors such as its aspirations for regional leadership, the influence of Turkish public opinion, and the ideological affinity with the Palestinian cause.

Humanitarian and Development Aid:

Turkey has been involved in providing humanitarian and development aid to the Palestinian territories, including Gaza. We discuss the significance of this assistance and its impact on the well-being of the Palestinian population.

Diplomatic Efforts:

Turkey has engaged in diplomatic efforts to promote Palestinian unity and peace in the region. We analyze these initiatives and their implications for the Israeli-Palestinian conflict.

Hosting Hamas Leaders:

Turkey has hosted Hamas leaders and provided them with a platform to engage with the international community. We explore the diplomatic and political ramifications of this hosting.

Challenges and Controversies:

The Turkey-Hamas relationship has not been without challenges, including criticism from other regional actors and the wider international community. We discuss how these challenges have affected both Turkey's policies and Hamas's international image.

Impact on Regional Politics:

Turkey's involvement with Hamas is part of a broader Turkish strategy in the Middle East. We analyze how this partnership fits into Turkey's regional ambitions and its relations with other actors.

Prospects for the Future:

As the Middle East continues to evolve, we consider the potential future scenarios for the Turkey-Hamas relationship and its implications for international relations in the region.

Conclusion:

The chapter provides a comprehensive examination of the multifaceted relationship between Hamas and Turkey, shedding light on the motivations, support, and diplomatic efforts that have characterized this partnership. It serves as a critical case study of how a state's involvement with a non-state actor like Hamas can influence the geopolitics of the Middle East.

8

Chapter 8: Gaza Blockade and Regional Actors: Dynamics of Isolation

Chapter Overview:
This chapter delves into the Gaza blockade and the impact it has on Hamas's alliances and interactions with regional actors. It explores the complex dynamics of isolation faced by Gaza and the implications for international relations.

Introduction:

The blockade of the Gaza Strip is a defining feature of the Israeli-Palestinian conflict. This chapter examines how the blockade has shaped the regional dynamics and alliances involving Hamas, other Palestinian factions, and key regional actors.

The Gaza Blockade: Historical and Humanitarian Context:

We provide a historical overview of the Gaza blockade, its origins, and the humanitarian challenges it has created for the people of Gaza.

The Impact on Hamas's Rule in Gaza:

The blockade has posed significant challenges to Hamas's governance in the Gaza Strip. We analyze how this isolation has influenced Hamas's strategies and alliances.

The Role of Egypt:

Egypt's role in controlling the Rafah border crossing and its relationship with Hamas is a crucial element of the Gaza blockade. We discuss the dynamics of this relationship and its implications.

Hamas's Interactions with Other Palestinian Factions:

The Gaza blockade has had implications for Hamas's interactions with other Palestinian factions, such as Fatah. We explore the complexities of intra-Palestinian relations in the context of the blockade.

Regional Actors and Humanitarian Aid:

Various regional actors, including Turkey and Qatar, have sought to provide humanitarian aid to Gaza. We analyze how these efforts have impacted the broader regional dynamics and Hamas's alliances.

Challenges and Tensions:

The Gaza blockade has led to tensions between Hamas and regional actors, including Egypt and other Arab states. We discuss how these tensions have influenced Hamas's international relations.

The Role of the United Nations and International Community:

The international community's involvement in addressing the Gaza blockade is a significant aspect of this chapter. We explore the efforts of international organizations and the implications for the Israeli-Palestinian conflict.

Gaza's Future and Implications for Hamas's Alliances:

We consider the potential scenarios for Gaza's future, including the lifting of the blockade, and how these scenarios might affect Hamas's alliances and its role in international relations.

Conclusion:

The chapter provides a comprehensive analysis of the Gaza blockade's impact on Hamas's alliances and interactions with regional actors. It highlights the challenges of isolation faced by Gaza and the broader implications for international relations in the Middle East.

9

Chapter 9: Hamas and the Palestinian Authority: Rivalry and Cooperation

C hapter Overview:
This chapter delves into the complex and often contentious relationship between Hamas and the Palestinian Authority (PA). It examines the rivalry, cooperation, and power struggles between these two entities and their implications for international relations.

Introduction:

The relationship between Hamas and the Palestinian Authority has been marked by a complex interplay of rivalry and cooperation. This chapter aims to provide insights into the dynamics of this relationship and how it impacts the broader context of international relations in the Palestinian territories.

Historical Roots of the Rivalry:

The rivalry between Hamas and the PA, particularly the Fatah faction, has deep historical roots, dating back to the early days of the Palestinian Authority. We provide an overview of the origins of this rivalry.

Power Struggles and Conflict:

The power struggles between Hamas and the PA have often manifested as political and territorial conflict, particularly in the Gaza Strip. We discuss the implications of these conflicts for both entities and for the broader Palestinian political landscape.

Cooperation and Reconciliation Attempts:

Despite their differences, there have been attempts at cooperation and reconciliation between Hamas and the PA. We examine the motivations behind these efforts and their outcomes.

External Mediation and International Actors:

International actors, including regional powers and Western countries, have played roles in mediating between Hamas and the PA. We discuss the impact of these mediation efforts on the relationship between the two entities and their implications for international relations.

The Unity Government:

The formation of a unity government in 2014 was a significant development in the Hamas-PA relationship. We analyze the challenges and opportunities presented by this unity government and its subsequent dissolution.

Security Coordination:

Security coordination between the PA and Israel has been a contentious issue, with implications for Hamas-PA relations. We explore the dynamics of this coordination and its impact on international perceptions of the Palestinian leadership.

Prospects for Reconciliation and Implications for International Relations:

We consider the prospects for future reconciliation between Hamas and the PA and how such reconciliation might impact the broader international relations of the Palestinian territories.

Conclusion:

The chapter provides a comprehensive analysis of the complex and often tumultuous relationship between Hamas and the Palestinian Authority. It highlights the power struggles, cooperation, and external mediation that have characterized this relationship and its implications for international relations in the Palestinian territories.

10

Chapter 10: U.S. and EU Policies Towards Hamas: Engagement or Isolation?

Chapter Overview:
This chapter focuses on the policies of the United States and the European Union (EU) towards Hamas. It explores the strategies of engagement or isolation that these Western actors have employed and the challenges they face in dealing with a designated terrorist organization.

Introduction:

The policies of the United States and the European Union towards Hamas have significant implications for the international standing of the organization. This chapter examines how Western actors have navigated the complexities of engaging with or isolating Hamas.

Designation as a Terrorist Organization:

Both the U.S. and the EU have designated Hamas as a terrorist organization. We provide context on this designation and its legal and political ramifications.

Engagement Efforts:

Despite the terrorist designation, some Western actors have attempted to engage with Hamas in various ways. We discuss diplomatic initiatives, indirect negotiations, and humanitarian efforts.

Challenges of Engagement:

Engaging with Hamas presents a set of challenges for Western actors, including concerns about legitimizing a group with a history of violence. We analyze these challenges and their impact on Western policies.

Isolation Policies:

Other Western actors, particularly the U.S., have adopted a policy of isolating Hamas. We examine the motivations behind this approach and its implications for international relations.

Humanitarian Aid and Development Assistance:

Even in the case of isolation, the provision of humanitarian aid and development assistance to the Palestinian territories remains a vital part of Western policy. We discuss how this aid is administered and its impact.

Regional Alliances and the Quartet:

Western actors have often coordinated their policies on Hamas through the Middle East Quartet, which includes the U.S., EU, UN, and Russia. We analyze the role of the Quartet in shaping Western policies.

Changes in Western Attitudes:

Western attitudes towards Hamas have evolved over time. We explore the factors that have contributed to shifts in policy, such as changes in leadership and the dynamics of the Israeli-Palestinian conflict.

Future Scenarios:

As the Middle East continues to change, we consider the potential future scenarios for Western policies towards Hamas and their implications for international relations in the region.

Conclusion:

This chapter provides a comprehensive analysis of the policies of the United States and the European Union towards Hamas. It highlights the challenges of engaging with or isolating a designated terrorist organization and the evolving nature of Western attitudes and policies.

11

Chapter 11: The Role of Non-State Actors: Networks, Alliances, and Challenges

Chapter Overview:

This chapter explores the role of non-state actors in international relations, with a specific focus on Hamas and its interactions with other non-state entities. It examines the networks and alliances that Hamas has formed with groups like Hezbollah and the challenges this poses to the international community.

Introduction:

In an increasingly interconnected and multipolar world, the influence of non-state actors has grown significantly. This chapter provides a framework for understanding the dynamics of non-state actors, focusing on the relationships that Hamas has forged with groups like Hezbollah.

Non-State Actors in International Relations:

We begin by discussing the changing landscape of international relations, which includes the increasing prominence of non-state actors. This shift has blurred the traditional lines between state and non-state entities.

Hamas and Hezbollah: A Complex Relationship:

We delve into the relationship between Hamas and Hezbollah, two prominent non-state actors in the Middle East. This includes their shared opposition to Israel and their interactions on political, military, and financial fronts.

Transnational Networks and Alliances:

The chapter explores the various transnational networks and alliances that Hamas has formed, not only with Hezbollah but also with other actors in the region. We discuss the implications of these alliances for international relations.

Challenges for the International Community:

The rise of non-state actors like Hamas and their interactions with other entities create challenges for the international community. We examine the difficulties in dealing with these actors and the limitations of traditional state-centric diplomacy.

Impact on Conflict Dynamics:

Hamas's interactions with non-state actors influence the dynamics of the Israeli-Palestinian conflict and the broader Middle East. We analyze how these relationships affect regional stability and the potential for peace.

Countering Non-State Actors:

Western countries and international organizations have sought to counter the influence of non-state actors like Hamas through various means, including sanctions and diplomatic efforts. We discuss the strategies employed to address this challenge.

The Broader Geopolitical Context:

Hamas's alliances with non-state actors are part of the broader regional power struggles in the Middle East. We explore how these alliances fit into the geopolitical puzzle of the region.

Future Scenarios:

As the international landscape continues to evolve, we consider potential future scenarios for the role of non-state actors like Hamas and their impact on international relations.

Conclusion:

The chapter provides an in-depth analysis of the role of non-state actors in international relations, using the interactions between Hamas and groups like Hezbollah as a case study. It highlights the challenges posed by non-state entities and their potential to shape regional and global dynamics.

12

Chapter 12: Future Prospects: Hamas and the Changing Landscape of International Relations

Chapter Overview:

In this final chapter, we explore the potential future scenarios for Hamas and its role in the ever-changing landscape of international relations. We examine the organization's adaptability, challenges it faces, and the implications of its actions on the global stage.

Introduction:

As the book approaches its conclusion, this chapter looks forward, contemplating the future prospects of Hamas and the international relations it will navigate in the years to come.

Adaptability and Resilience:

Hamas has demonstrated a remarkable ability to adapt to changing circumstances, both regionally and globally. We discuss how the organization's resilience and flexibility have allowed it to remain a relevant force in international politics.

Regional Dynamics:

The dynamics of the Middle East are continuously evolving. We explore how shifts in regional politics, conflicts, and alliances may impact Hamas's role and its relationships with neighboring states.

Palestinian Politics:

Hamas's place in Palestinian politics remains a central issue. We analyze how it will continue to interact with the Palestinian Authority, Fatah, and the broader political landscape.

International Engagement:

Hamas has made efforts to engage with the international community, despite its terrorist designation. We discuss the prospects for these diplomatic initiatives and the potential for international recognition.

External Influences:

We examine how the involvement of external actors, including regional powers and Western countries, will shape the future of Hamas and its alliances.

Security Challenges:

The security landscape in the Middle East poses ongoing challenges. We explore how Hamas will address these challenges and maintain its armed resistance capabilities.

Peace Prospects:

The chapter considers the potential for peace in the Israeli-Palestinian conflict and how Hamas's role may evolve in a future peace process.

Conclusion:

The final chapter concludes by summarizing the key points discussed throughout the book and offering insights into the multifaceted nature of Hamas and its place in international relations. It emphasizes the importance of continued analysis and adaptation in understanding the evolving role of Hamas in the ever-changing landscape of global politics.